DISCARD

ancient
egyptians

SERIES EDITOR   DAVID SALARIYA
BOOK EDITOR   APRIL McCROSKIE

First American Edition 1996 by
Franklin Watts
A Division of Grolier Publishing
Sherman Turnpike
Danbury, Connecticut 06816

© THE SALARIYA BOOK COMPANY LTD MCMXCVI

Library of Congress Cataloging-in-Publication Data
Kerr, Daisy.
   Ancient Egyptians / written by Daisy Kerr : illustrated by John James.
     p. cm. – (Worldwise)
   ISBN 0-531-14401-1 (lib. bdg.)   0-531-15294-4 (pbk.)
   1. Egypt – Civilization – To 332 B.C. – Juvenile literature.
I. James, John, 1959– ill. II. Title. III. Series.
DT61.K445   1996
932' .01 – dc20   95-46729
                                   CIP AC

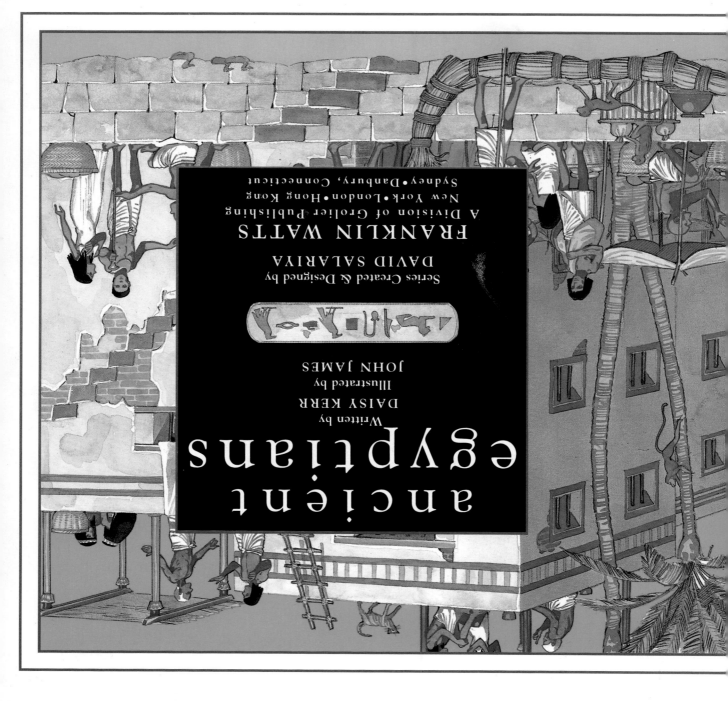

ancient egyptians

Written by
DAISY KERR

Illustrated by
JOHN JAMES

Series Created & Designed by
DAVID SALARIYA

FRANKLIN WATTS
A Division of Grolier Publishing
New York • London • Hong Kong
Sydney • Danbury, Connecticut

CONTENTS

The ancient Egyptians

lived in north Africa. From around 3100 B.C., they developed a rich, powerful civilization that lasted for thousands of years. Egyptian farmers grew many crops and craftworkers built magnificent monuments. Egyptian Pharaohs led mighty armies and scientists made many important discoveries in mathematics and technology.

Egyptian power collapsed when Roman armies invaded in 30 B.C. But Egyptian skills and traditions survived for many more years.

Egypt lay at the crossroads of several important trade routes linking north Africa with Arabia, the Middle East, and lands around the Mediterranean Sea.

Over 90 percent of Egypt is desert. The only fertile, well-watered land is in the northern delta region, and along the banks of the Nile River.

Ancient Egyptians

divided their country into two different regions – "Deshret" (meaning Red Land, the desert) and "Kemet" (meaning Black Land, for the black soil).

Deshret was a dry, stony desert. No one could live there, but it was rich in minerals. Tough Egyptian laborers were sent to quarry granite and limestone for statues and temples, copper for weapons and tools, and gold, turquoise, and carnelian for jewelry.

In Kemet you could see villages and fields of rich, black mud along the banks of the Nile River. All living things in Egypt depended on the Nile.

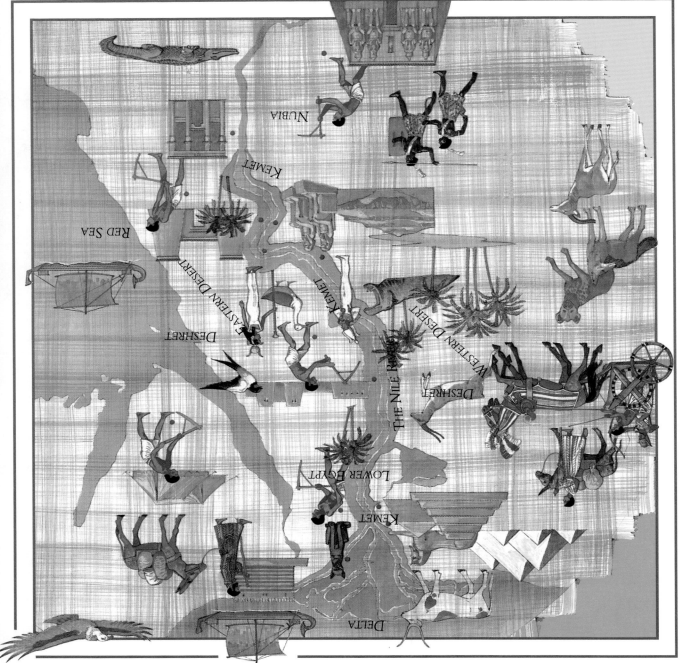

THE LAND OF EGYPT

Every year, in July, Nile floods covered the fields with water and rich, fertile mud.

In October, the flood waters retreated. Farmers plowed the fields and sowed seeds.

Workers dug new irrigation channels to bring more river water to the fields.

In April, the corn was ready to harvest. Farmers cut it with flint-toothed sickles.

An Egyptian farmer's year

was divided into three seasons – floods, seed sprouting and harvest. At flood time their fields were under water, so they could not work on the land. They had to work on government building projects such as a new road or a pyramid tomb. Egyptian farmers grew wheat to make bread, and also fruit and vegetables like figs, grapes, onions, and garlic. Some farmers grew palm trees for thatch; others grew flax to make linen cloth.

Digging stick

Some fields were plowed by oxen. Others were cultivated using digging sticks. Seed was scattered by hand, then trampled into the mud by animals.

THE FARMER'S YEAR

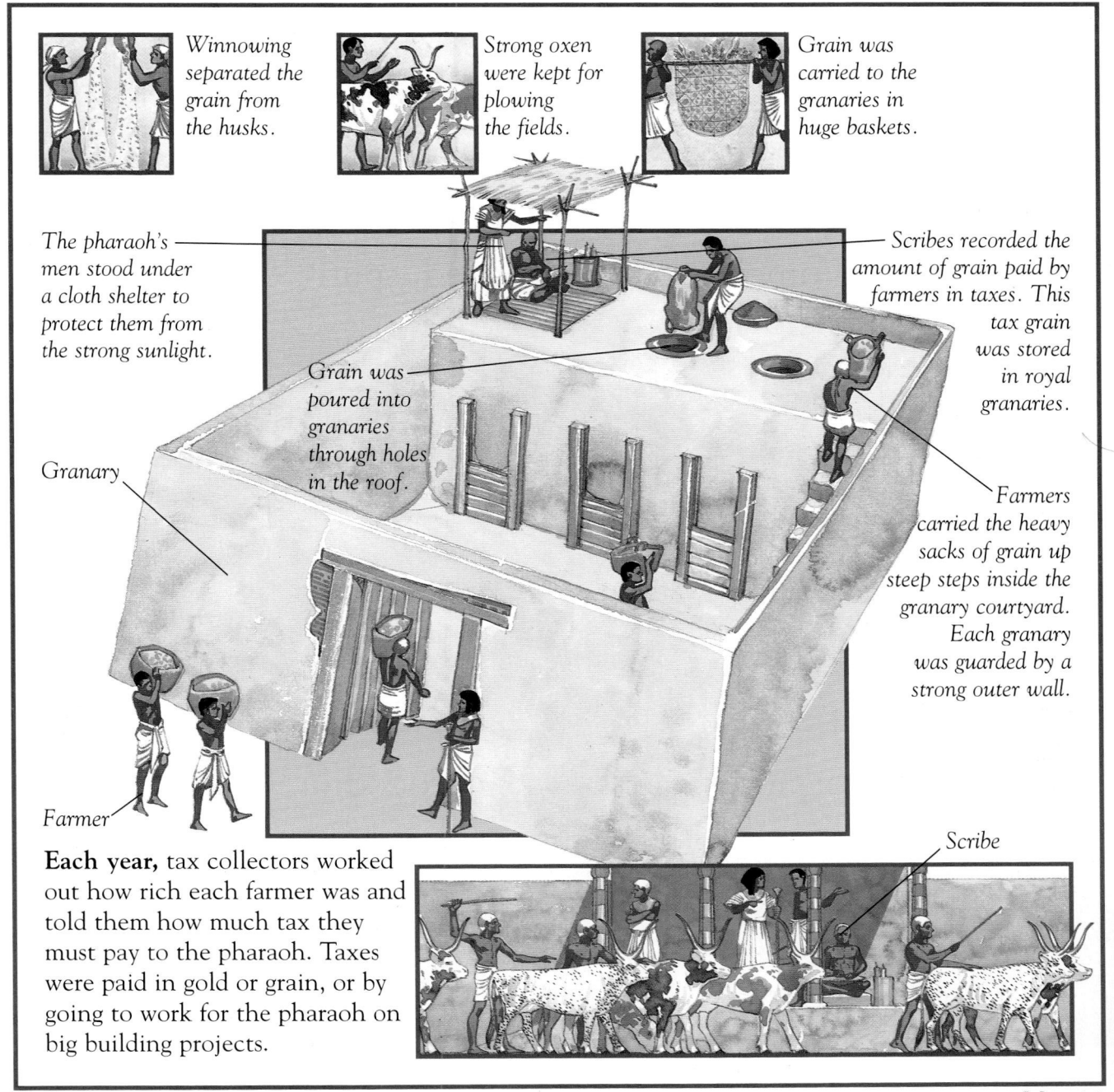

Winnowing separated the grain from the husks.

Strong oxen were kept for plowing the fields.

Grain was carried to the granaries in huge baskets.

The pharaoh's men stood under a cloth shelter to protect them from the strong sunlight.

Scribes recorded the amount of grain paid by farmers in taxes. This tax grain was stored in royal granaries.

Grain was poured into granaries through holes in the roof.

Granary

Farmers carried the heavy sacks of grain up steep steps inside the granary courtyard. Each granary was guarded by a strong outer wall.

Farmer

Scribe

Each year, tax collectors worked out how rich each farmer was and told them how much tax they must pay to the pharaoh. Taxes were paid in gold or grain, or by going to work for the pharaoh on big building projects.

Egyptian families provided

jobs, love and security for their members.
Village men worked in the fields or in craft
workshops. Women cooked, cleaned, spun
thread, wove cloth, and brewed beer at
home. Rich women organized servants, too.

Egyptians married young, but many people
died before they were 30. Men were killed
in battle and women died in childbirth.
Egyptian doctors used herbal remedies, but
anyone might catch a deadly disease, be
stung by a scorpion, or eaten by a crocodile.

Egyptians married
for love and for
money, too.
A rich bride
was highly prized.

Laws protected
women. They
could get a divorce
if their husbands
treated them badly.

Most children
were taught skills
at home. Boys
learned farming
or craft work,
girls learned
household and
child-care skills.

*The Egyptians did not
use money. Families
bartered (swapped)
goods at the market.*

Egyptian families
hoped to have lots
of children, to help
run their houses,
workshops and farms.

Ordinary houses had earth

floors and plaster-covered walls. Most had two or three rooms and a courtyard, used for cooking. Furniture was simple, too – a bed, a few chairs or stools, some wooden chests, and pottery jars for storing olive oil, grain, and wine. Rich families had more luxurious homes, built on two or three floors, each having separate bathrooms.

Clay model of a house, showing doorway, window, courtyard, outside stairs, and flat roof. Models like this were placed in tombs.

House belonging to a skilled workman employed to build grand tombs for pharaohs around 1350 B.C.

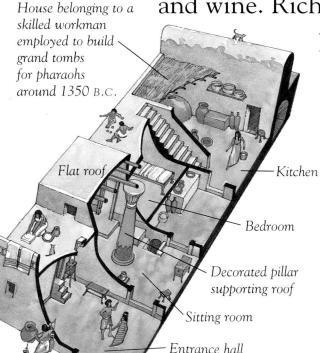

Flat roof

Kitchen

Bedroom

Decorated pillar supporting roof

Sitting room

Entrance hall

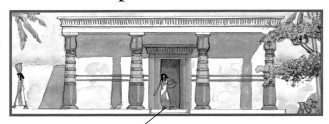

Grand entrance porch of a house built for a noble family around 1320 B.C. The house had many big rooms and a large garden.

Egyptian builders also constructed massive palaces, temples, and pyramid tombs. Turn the page to see a pyramid being built.

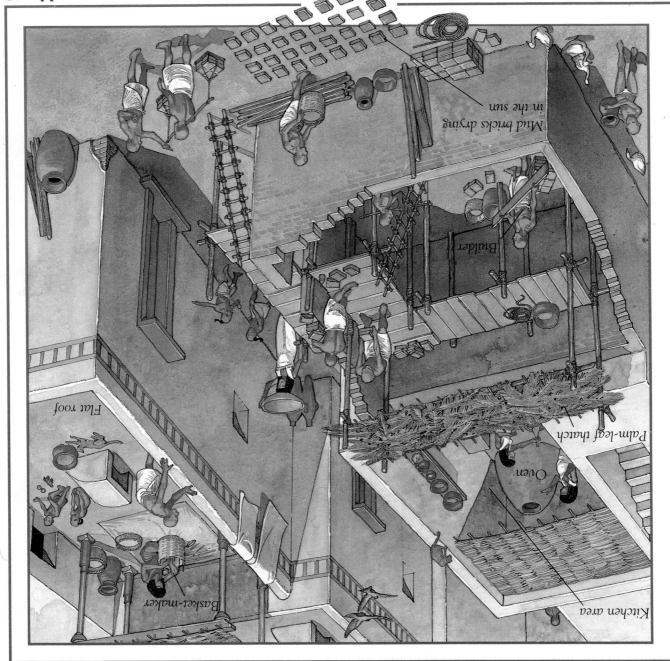

HOUSES AND HOMES

Mud bricks drying in the sun

Builder

Palm-leaf thatch

Flat roof

Oven

Basket-maker

Kitchen area

Courtiers and other rich people wore long tunics of fine pleated linen, which felt cool and comfortable in Egypt's hot weather. They also liked to wear elegant wigs, and jewelry made of gold, turquoise, and lapis lazuli – a blue stone.

Left to right: Overseer; Irrigation manager; Controller of state granaries; Chief steward; Director of building works; Army commander; Controller of nome (province); Chief scribe; Courtier.

Egypt was ruled by powerful kings, called pharaohs. The pharaoh was thought to be the son of god and the chief priest. He was the army commander and head of the government, giving orders to officials and scribes. He supervised law and order, tax collection, food supplies and trade, irrigation, and mining. The pharaoh also held audiences at his splendid royal court, where he listened to requests from top officials, nobles, and visitors from distant lands.

PHARAOH'S DAY

Making offerings of food and drink to gods and goddesses in the temples.

Listening to reports about the country from the vizier (head of administration).

Inspecting major public works – pyramids, roads, ditches and canals.

The Pharaoh was also a war leader. It was his duty to plan campaigns and command the army. The most famous warrior pharaoh was Ramses II (1279-1213 B.C.).

The word "pharaoh" comes from *perr-aa*, which means "great house."

Pharaohs received tribute – presents of rich treasures like gold and cedarwood – from conquered lands.

Documents authorized by the pharaoh were stamped with his seal.

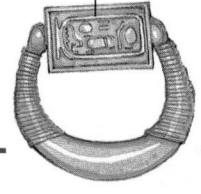

Musicians entertained the Pharaoh and his guests with songs.

Favorite instruments included the flute, zither, and harp.

Dancers made music with clappers, bells, and kitharas.

On hunting trips, Egyptians chased water birds, snakes, and sometimes crocodiles.

Double flute player   *Kithara player*   *Harp player*   *Lyre player*

The Egyptians enjoyed their leisure time.

Pharaohs and nobles held great banquets, where they entertained guests with delicious food, music, and dancing. Ordinary people also enjoyed dances and songs. They had picnics and hunting trips beside the river, too.

Honored guests   *Perfumed wax*   *Pharaoh*

Women guests were offered cones of perfumed wax that melted in their hair.

The Pharaoh and his guests were entertained by dancers and acrobats. Many dances were full of leaps, handstands, and somersaults.

Guests ate roast duck, stewed deer, lettuce and onion salads, and date and honey cake.

Pharaoh's servant

Egyptian toys. These painted clay rattles were filled with seeds and beads.

Egyptians enjoyed listening to storytellers, watching jugglers and magicians, and playing board games like "senet" (similar to modern checkers). Children played with rattles, tops, dolls, and wooden animals on wheels.

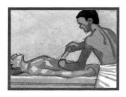

The lungs, liver, intestines, and stomach were taken out of the body to stop it from rotting.

The body was packed with natron (soda) and left for 40 days in a natron-filled trough to dry out.

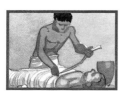

Finally, the body was wrapped in resin-soaked bandages to keep the dried flesh and bones in place. If a bit of body dropped off or rotted away, the embalmers replaced it with linen pads and bits of wood.

The ancient Egyptians

feared death and wanted to live forever. They believed that if a dead person's body was preserved, their spirit would be preserved too, giving them everlasting life.

At first, the Egyptians preserved bodies by burying them in the desert. The dry sand stopped them from rotting away. Later, pharaohs and rich people paid to have their bodies preserved as mummies by embalming. The word "mummy" comes from the Arabic word for black tar – people thought mummies looked as if they were covered in tar. The Egyptians also mummified their favorite animals, especially pet cats. They buried them in special temple cemeteries.

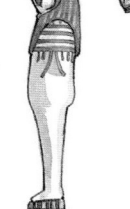

Amulets (small carvings) were placed between the layers of bandages. Egyptians believed these helped preserve the body.

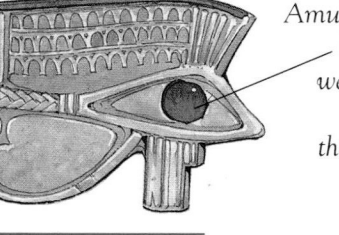

Amulets shaped like an eye were thought to protect the mummy.

The mummy case was painted with many magic spells, written in hieroglyphs, to help the mummy's spirit in the life after death.

The body was wrapped in layers of shrouds, then placed in a mummy-shaped inner coffin. Often this was painted with a portrait of the dead person's face.

Turn the page to see inside a mummy case.

Once inside the inner coffin, the mummy was placed in a strong, rot-proof outer case. This might be made of wood or stone.

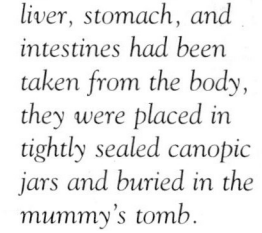

After the lungs, liver, stomach, and intestines had been taken from the body, they were placed in tightly sealed canopic jars and buried in the mummy's tomb.

Pharaohs' bodies were ferried across the Nile River from the east bank, where the royal palaces were, to the west bank – the City of the Dead. Priests and mourners went along, too.

The funeral boat was made of cedar wood. It was about 147 feet (45 m) long, and powered by rowers. It was guided by double steering oars.

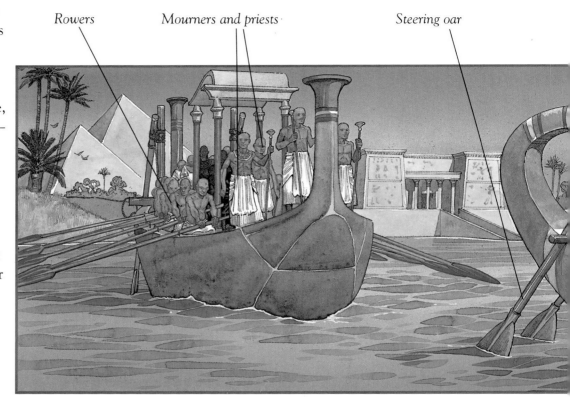

Rowers

Mourners and priests

Steering oar

Funerals took place on the west bank of the Nile. Once a mummy was buried, its spirit began a new life in the City of the Dead. Tombs were decorated with paintings of the dead person hunting, worshiping the gods, and enjoying family life. Tombs had everything the

dead person might need – food and drink,
clothes, weapons, and games. Models of
houses, boats, farm animals, servants, and
companions were also placed in the tomb,
so the dead person could enjoy these too.

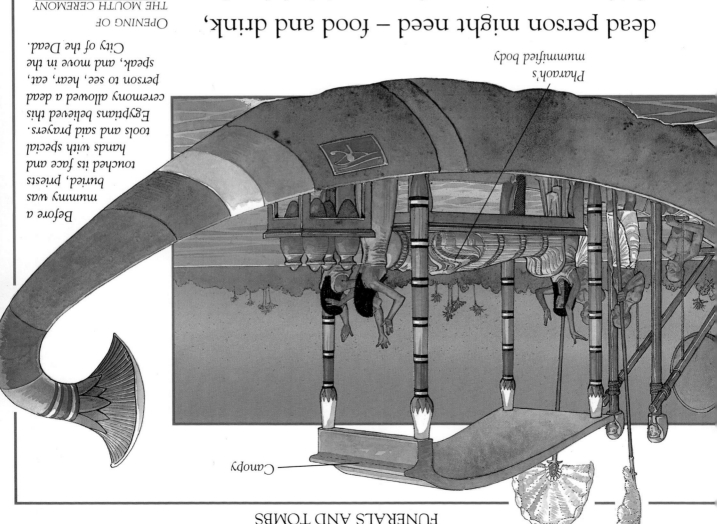

OPENING OF
THE MOUTH CEREMONY

Before a
mummy was
buried, priests
touched its face and
hands with special
tools and said prayers.
Egyptians believed this
ceremony allowed a dead
person to see, hear, eat,
speak, and move in the
City of the Dead.

Pharaoh's
mummified body

Canopy

FUNERALS AND TOMBS

Hieroglyphs

Priests and scribes could read and write hieroglyphs – a system of picture writing with over 700 symbols.

Boys who wanted to be priests had to study hard at school. They were beaten if they did not listen.

The Egyptians worshiped

many gods and goddesses. They built temples to honor them, where priests and pharaohs offered clothes, food, and water three times a day. They carved to show their many forms like Horus, the hawklike sky god, Sekhmet, the lion-headed goddess of battle, or Bastet, a proud cat. Some were worshiped in only one place, like crocodile god Sobek, who lived in the river. Others, like sun god Amun-Re, were worshiped everywhere.

Shrine

Temple

Temples were homes for gods and goddesses. Each temple had a shrine – a special holy place, where the spirit of the god or goddess lived. This spirit was represented by a huge statue.

On festival days (right), statues were carried through the streets by priests. Often, the statues were hidden inside a shrine – they were thought to be too holy for people to see.

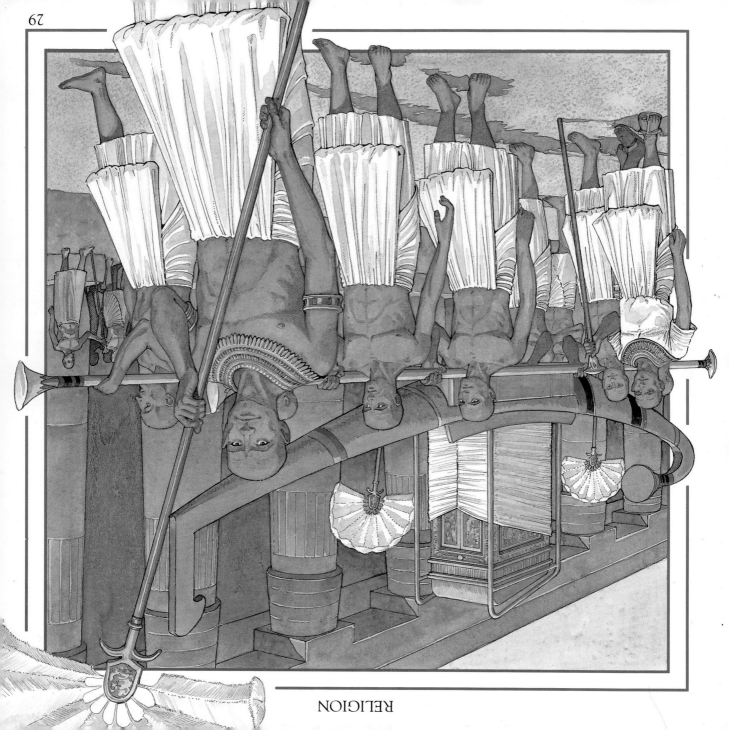

We know about Egyptian towns because their remains, like Kahun (built around 1895 B.C.) and Deir el Medina (built around 1350 B.C.) have been excavated (dug up).

Potters

Carpenters

Craftworkers

used simple tools – flint drills, wooden mallets and bronze saws. Yet their monuments have survived for almost 5,000 years. Most artists and craftspeople worked for the government, building and decorating massive palaces and tombs. Other skilled people worked at home, making sandals, molding pottery, or carving wood. Gold workers, wig makers, jewelers, and glass blowers made and sold their goods in towns.

Nile River

Rooftop shelter

Sandal makers

Children helping parents

Spice seller

Palm tree leaves used as thatch

Cloth hung over balcony to bleach in the sun

Basket makers

31

Scribes were officials who recorded events, helped collect taxes, and wrote down the Pharaoh's orders.

Governors of nomes (provinces) had the power to make a man work for the pharaoh or join the army.

Criminals were punished severely. Beating by lawcourt officials was the most common penalty.

Around 3100 B.C., Pharaoh Menes united the two earlier kingdoms of upper and lower Egypt into one large nation. Then the Egyptians fought and conquered peoples, in what is now present-day Libya, Syria, and Iraq. Egyptian troops were tough, well-fed, and fit. Soldiers fought on foot, using bows and arrows, spears, axes, and clubs.

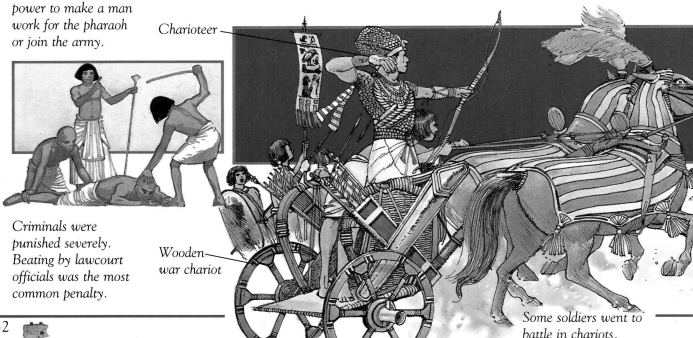

Charioteer

Wooden war chariot

Some soldiers went to battle in chariots.

Battles were bloody and if enemies were captured, they became slaves.

Egypt was difficult to govern. There were few roads, and travel by river was slow. Even urgent messages could take weeks to arrive. So, pharaohs divided the kingdom into provinces, called "nomes," and relied on governors to help them rule.

Spear

Battle axe

Short wool or linen kilt

Shield

Bare feet

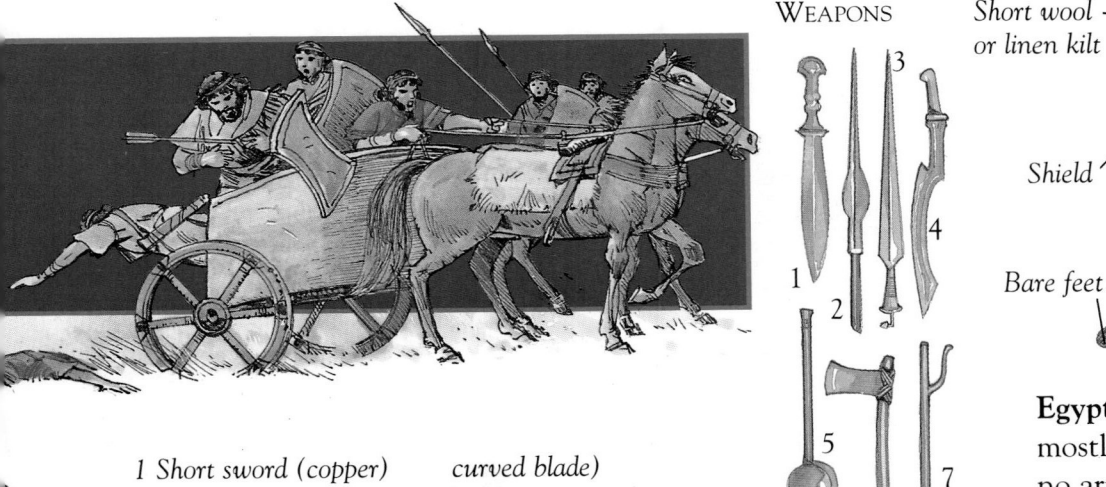

WEAPONS

1 Short sword (copper)
2 Spear head (bronze)
3 Spear head (bronze)
4 Scimitar (sword with curved blade)
5 Club with sharp point
6 Battle axe
7 Wooden club

Egyptian soldiers fought mostly on foot. They had no armor. Instead, they defended themselves with large wooden shields.

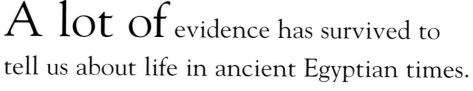

A lot of evidence has survived to tell us about life in ancient Egyptian times. The pharaohs' magnificent pyramid tombs still stand. There are wall paintings, carvings and statues, hieroglyphic inscriptions, and temples and palaces. Books written on papyrus (paper made from reeds) by Egyptian scribes tell us about ancient beliefs and ceremonies. We can also learn about the ancient Egyptians from travelers like the Greek writer Herodotus, who visited the country around 500 B.C.

Ancient Greeks and Romans who visited Egypt between 500 B.C.-A.D. 200 wrote descriptions of Egyptian civilization.

French army commander Napoleon Bonaparte invaded Egypt in 1789. He took many Egyptian remains back to France.

The Rosetta Stone (unearthed 1799) helped scholars learn how to read hieroglyphs. It has the same message in three different scripts – hieroglyphs, demotic (everyday Egyptian language, which used letters), and ancient Greek.

Two famous Egyptian names in hieroglyphs and letters.

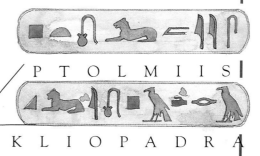

P T O L M I I S

K L I O P A D R A

Archaeologists have used modern remote-control robot cameras to investigate narrow passageways deep inside pyramids and tombs.

Computers can be used to "reconstruct" statues and buildings that have been damaged over the centuries. A computer can show what damaged stonework would have looked like when new.

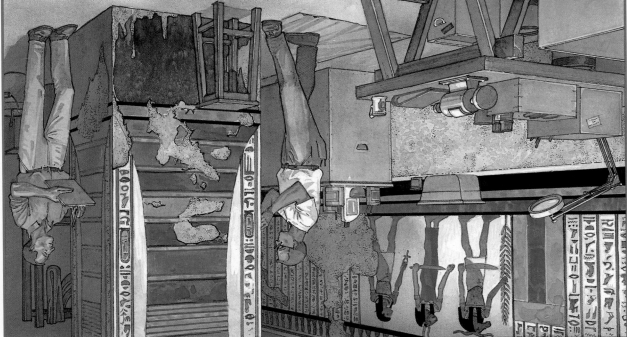

Tourism has damaged many ancient Egyptian remains. Moisture from visitors' breath and sweat has rotted fragile objects preserved in dry tombs for over 3000 years.

Today, archaeologists use scientific techniques and modern materials (like plastics and new types of glue) to try to preserve ancient Egyptian remains. Without this expert conservation work, many old wall paintings and stone carvings would crumble away.

The boy pharaoh, Tutankhamen, died around 1352 B.C. His tomb survived untouched. It was discovered in 1922, and shows us how rich Egyptian civilization was.

Four shrines made of gold-covered wood, one inside the other

Antechamber, containing carved bed and guardian statues

Annex

Gold coffin found in Tutankhamen's tomb. It is decorated with colored glass and carnelian (a red semi-precious stone).

The last

pyramid was built around 2150 B.C. Later pharaohs were buried in tombs in cliffs in the Valley of the Kings. These tombs were filled with treasures, but, in spite of hidden entrances and armed guards, most were robbed.

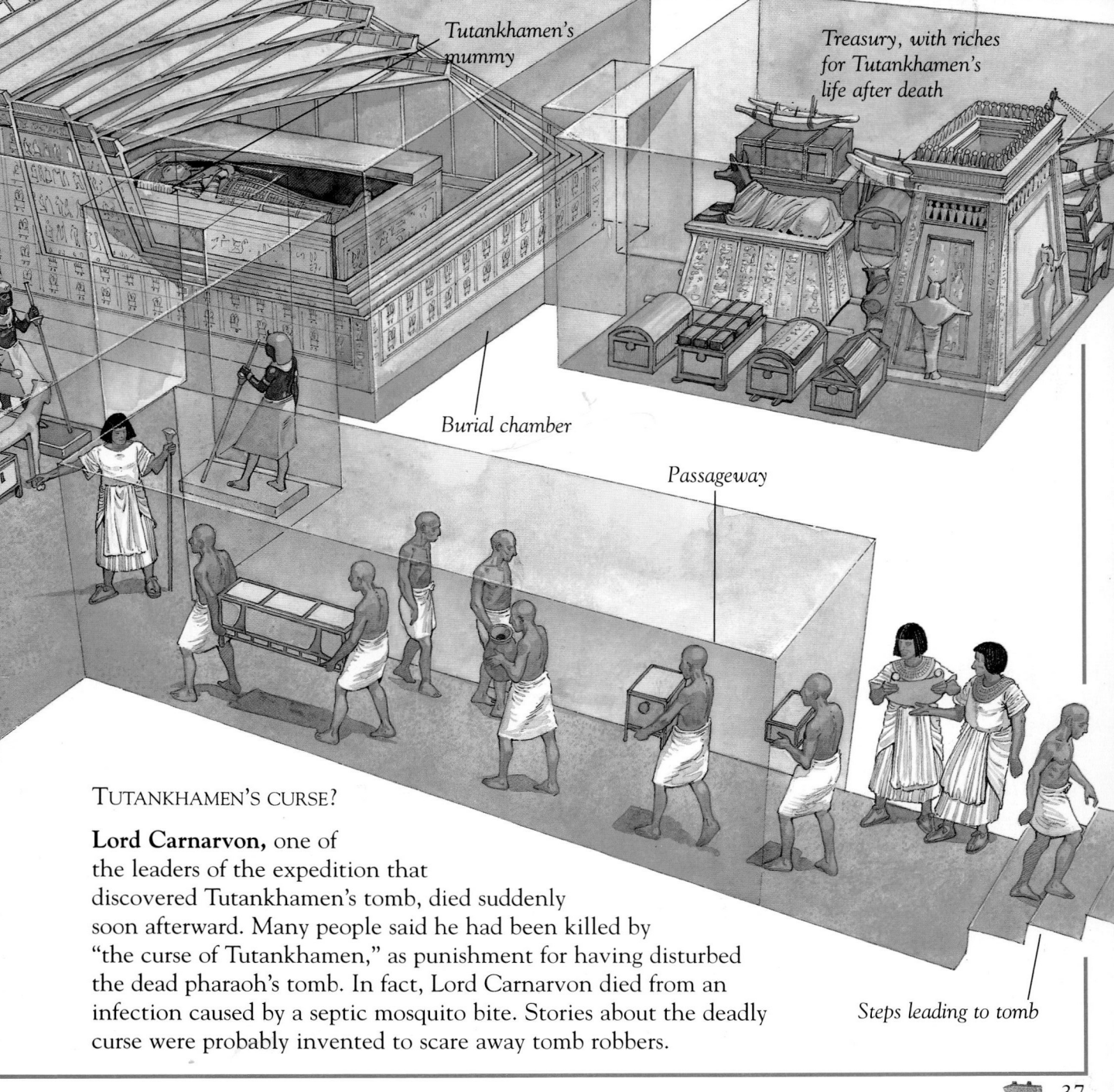

Tutankhamen's mummy

Treasury, with riches for Tutankhamen's life after death

Burial chamber

Passageway

TUTANKHAMEN'S CURSE?

Lord Carnarvon, one of the leaders of the expedition that discovered Tutankhamen's tomb, died suddenly soon afterward. Many people said he had been killed by "the curse of Tutankhamen," as punishment for having disturbed the dead pharaoh's tomb. In fact, Lord Carnarvon died from an infection caused by a septic mosquito bite. Stories about the deadly curse were probably invented to scare away tomb robbers.

Steps leading to tomb

USEFUL WORDS

Archaeologist
Someone who finds out about the past by studying its objects and buildings.

Amulet Small object believed to guard against evil. Often put inside mummies.

Canopic jars Containers to hold the lungs, liver, stomach, and intestines of a body being mummified.

Embalming Preserving by soaking in resin or by wrapping in resin-soaked bandages.

Hieroglyphs
Picture writing, used by ancient Egyptian scribes. At first, each hieroglyph showed an object. Later, hieroglyphs came to stand for sounds, like letters in our alphabet.

Irrigation
Bringing water to dry land.

Mummified Made into a mummy.

Natron A type of soda, found in the desert lands of Egypt. Used to dry dead bodies.

Papyrus A type of reed that grows beside the Nile River. It was used by Egyptians to make paper.

Pharaoh The ancient Egyptian word for king.

Scribes Government officials trained in reading, writing, and keeping records.

Shrine Holy place where the statue of a god or goddess was kept.

Shroud Cloth used to wrap dead bodies.

Vizier The pharaoh's chief minister.

INDEX

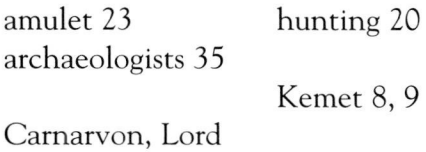